SUPER STRATEGIES

(Whole Language Activities in Children's Literature)

by
Celeste Bingham and Suzanne Sage

Publishers
T.S. Denison & Co., Inc.
Minneapolis, Minnesota 55431

Standard Book Number: 513-01942-1
Copyright © 1988 by T.S. Denison & Co., Inc.
Minneapolis, Minnesota 55431

INTRODUCTION

Super Strategies is designed to assist the teacher in creating a Total Language Arts Environment in the classroom. The activities provided are applicable to most reading selections whether from a basal text or literature. Wonderful ideas are provided for: Journal Writing, Reading Logs, Writing Folders, Silent Reading, and so much more. *Super Strategies* is filled with activities that encourage creative thinking, risk taking, problem solving and a whole learning experience.

This book is designed for the teacher who . . .

1) Uses a basal reading text.
2) Uses a basal reading text combined with literature selections; trade books, magazines, newspapers, etc.
3) Uses literature selections exclusively in a Whole Language Program.

The activities are divided into three sections; Vocabulary, Pre-Reading and Post-Reading.

VOCABULARY ACTIVITIES explore word meaning within the context rather than in isolation. They encourage children to internalize the words and discover new meanings.

PRE-READING ACTIVITIES center around estimating, prediction and problem-solving.

POST-READING ACTIVITIES allows the children to summarize, compare, interpret and evaluate.

The activities are designed to be general rather than specific in nature. They are applicable to any selection or theme and require a minimum of teacher preparation and materials. In addition they are easily adaptable for younger and older children. These activities are teacher-tested and have been worked and reworked. It is up to you to take these ideas and make them work for you.

DEDICATION
This book is dedicated to our students past and present who have served as guinea pigs as we developed and revised our ideas. Special thanks to Cheryl N. for her support and advice.

CONTENTS

* Indicates reproducible activity pages.

LANGUAGE ARTS ENVIRONMENT

This section has been included to show how to create a Language Arts Environment. The authors feel it is significant to provide opportunities where the child is free to express ideas and opinions in a variety of ways including listening, speaking, reading and writing. Children in this environment are encouraged to be risk takers, capable of defending the answer they feel is right. There are seldom right or wrong answers.

In creating a Language Arts Environment the children are surrounded by language. Emphasis is taken away from reading and language as separate subjects. These areas are now integrated to form a Language Arts block of time.

ELEMENTS OF A LANGUAGE ARTS ENVIRONMENT

STUDENT TEXT
These are the materials the children are reading during the Language Arts time. This may be a basal text or literature selections. Literature selections may include trade books; fiction, nonfiction, poetry, plays, biographies, newspapers, magazines, "how to" books, maps, wordless picture books, etc. Materials can be selected around a particular theme or topic; Dinosaurs, Fairy Tales, "You Don't Have to Be Big to Be a Giant." Activities are focused upon a chosen theme.

SILENT READING
This is an opportunity for the children to look at or read self selected materials for an uninterrupted amount of time. Children are not accountable to the teacher for what has been read. It is suggested that this be done daily for a period of 10 to 20 minutes.

TEACHER READING
Materials to be read orally to the class are selected by the teacher. An Author of the Month (week) can be highlighted to introduce the children to the work of a particular writer. Another method for selection is to have the books thematically related to the student text. This may be a book that is too difficult for the children to read themselves. Old favorites and classics are wonderful choices also. This should be done daily for 15 to 20 minutes.

JOURNALS

This is a booklet in which the children and teacher carry on a written dialogue. The children may begin the dialogue with "Dear Ms./Mr. _____." This provides an opportunity for the children to express their feelings and share experiences with the teacher. The teacher responds by writing a comment in the journal and tries to illicit further writing by asking questions. Frequency of this activity is up to the teacher's discretion.

EXAMPLE:

Dear Ms. Smith,
    Yesterday my family and I went to the mountains. We went camping with my cousins. It was fun. We roasted marshmallows. Have you ever been camping?
                                        Love,
                                        Bobby

Dear Bobby,
    It sure sounds like you had fun. I used to go camping with my family when I was a kid. What other vacations have you been on?
                                        Ms. Smith

READING LOGS

These are booklets of blank, lined paper where the children can respond to what has been read. A good number of the following activities can be recorded in the log. Logs offer a concise and flexible format for the children's work in reading. They help condense the amount of correcting for the teacher by keeping most of the paperwork in one place.

EXAMPLES:

"In your reading logs write five things you can do with a friend and five things you can do by yourself. When you are done pick your favorite from each list and draw a picture of it." (Introduction for a story on friends.)

"After reading Chapter Three, make a list of the new characters that were introduced and draw a picture of one of the characters."

"In your reading log, copy and complete the sentence 'My favorite things to do with my Grandmother are _____ and _____.' "

"Pretend that you are the author and in your reading log make a new last page for the story and draw a new picture."

WRITING FOLDERS

These are file folders with the child's name on them. Inside are several sheets of blank, lined paper. Time should be set aside daily for 15 to 45 minutes to allow the children time to work on original stories on any subject they wish.

There are several steps of the writing process; Getting the Idea, Writing, Peer Editing/Meetings, Re-writing, Meeting, and Publishing.

1) *GETTING THE IDEA* - Children may have their own ideas to get them started. To help those who don't, the teacher can provide ideas or the class can brainstorm ideas by listing story topics on the board.

2) *WRITING* - At this stage, children are writing down their ideas in story form. They are focused on creating the story rather than on spelling, punctuation and grammar.

3) *PEER EDITING/MEETINGS* - There should be communication between the teacher and the children at all stages of the writing process. Each child will be paired with another who will be his peer editor. The children are kept accountable for their writing by meeting in editing groups. These groups may be from 4 to 8 children. The size of the group will determine the amount of time. The children bring a story that they wish published to the group meeting. Not all stories that are written will be published.

Within the groups, children meet with the teacher and take turns reading their stories. Children have the opportunity to share their ideas and constructive comments with the author of the story. This aids the author in completing or revising their story. The teacher is able to monitor the children's *progress.* While a group is meeting, the rest of the children are working independently on their own writing.

When the children have questions during writing time or have completed a draft they meet with their editing partner. The editing partner reviews the story and helps the author make corrections. The teacher may want to meet individually with the author to review corrections.

4) *RE-WRITING* - After meeting with their editing partner the child decides whether or not to accept the changes suggested.The Story is then re-written or revised.

5) *MEETING* - The child brings their rewritten story to meet and discuss with the teacher. The teacher helps the child make final corrections in spelling, punctuation and grammar. The child moves to the publishing stage from here.

6) *PUBLISHING* - How the story is published depends on the child and materials provided from the teacher. The writing is put into book form including illustrations. It can be bound, stapled, laminated, or any other method of book making. Completed books can be read to the class by the author and put into the class library to be read by the other children. Besides being put into book form, writings can be published and put on a display board of "published works."

ORAL LANGUAGE

An essential part of a Language Arts Environment is Oral Language. Children should have many opportunities to interact and share their ideas in a non-threatening environment. Oral Language activities enable the teacher to measure the children's understanding.

Children are encouraged to participate in group conversation, dialogues with partners, brainstorming sessions and class discussions. Brainstorming is a method used to collect ideas in an informal way. It helps children to generate new ideas by incorporating the thoughts of others. The teacher may ask, "What do you know about...?" or "When you see the word _____ what do you think of?" All answers are accepted and usually recorded.

The Language Arts Environment may appear to be overwhelming. It may be implemented gradually. The diversity of the class and each teaching style will determine which elements will work best for you. Take these ideas, rework, adapt and revise them to suit your own personal needs.

VOCABULARY ACTIVITIES

In Context

1. Use pre-selected vocabulary words that you or the children feel are important to the meaning of the story.

2. Write each word on a flashcard.

3. Find the sentence or phrase in the story where the word appears. Write this on a large chart, overhead or chalkboard, omitting the vocabulary word.

4. As a group, discuss which word goes into the blank on the chart. Any response is acceptable as long as it conveys meaning and the student can defend his/her choice.

For Example:

Words on
    Cards

1) He walked up and down on the _____ for a long time.

path
meadow
riverbank
porch

2) Bob ran up the _____ to Tim's house.

3) They walked across a large _____.

4) A turtle came along the _____.

All of these words will make sense in each of these sentences. The class will need to decide which answer they feel is the best answer. As they read the selection they will discover the meaning that was intended by the author.

Guess and Check

(Use with the reproducible activity sheet found on page 11.)

1. Draw a picture or write a sentence of what you think the word means.

2. Share and discuss with a partner or the class.

3. After reading, draw a picture and/or write a sentence to show what the word means. Compare with the original prediction.

Guess That Word

Materials: Cards with vocabulary words written on them.

This activity is best suited to words within a content area that have already been introduced.

1. The teacher selects a student to be the contestant.

2. The teacher places the word card out of the contestant's view.

3. The rest of the students give 1 to 3 word clues as to what the word means.

4. The contestant tries to guess the word using the given clues. It is up to the teacher's discretion to limit the amount of clues that can be given or set a time limit.

5. Select a new contestant.

Guess & Check

GUESS ?   CHECK √

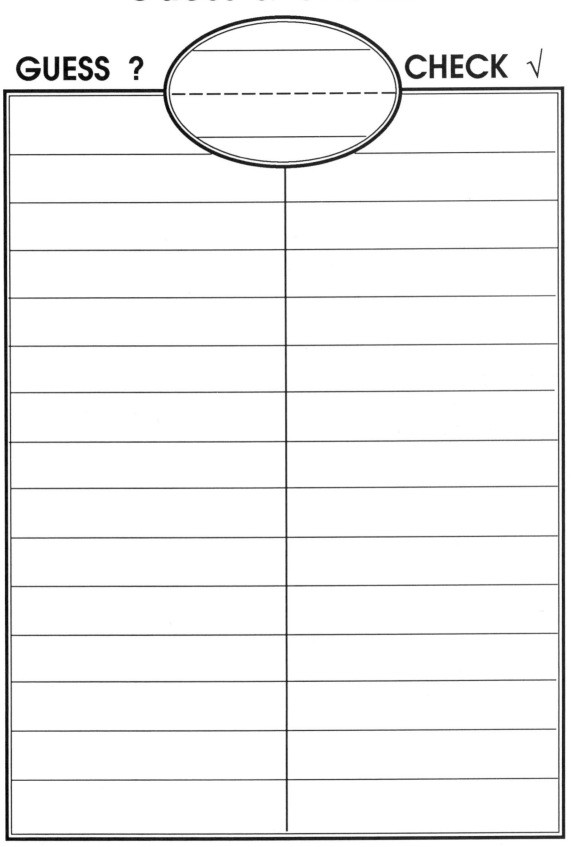

Name _____

Sorting Words

(Use with the the reproducible activity sheet found on page 13.)

1. Words can be sorted many different ways.
    a. Persons, places, things, actions, and words that describe.
    b. Words that go-together. Provide the students with words that they have to justify, such as; "I think blossoms and nature go-together because blossoms are flowers and flowers are a part of nature." By using words on flashcards, or pictures for younger students, the children can sort the vocabulary words on the chalkrails or by using a pocket chart.

Predict-A-Word

1. The teacher will show the children pictures from the selection that will help to tell the story.

2. The children predict what words they think will be important in the story based on the pictures they saw. This can be done by:
    a) Oral class discussion.
    b) Individual lists.
    c) Group lists (2 to 4 children).
    d) Whole class list.

The teacher may want to record all responses to be compared after reading the story.

Variation: The teacher would prepare a word list. The children would pull words from the list based on the pictures that they saw.

Sell-A-Word

Have the children make a poster, banner, or sign to advertize a certain word. The word may be either child or teacher selected. The ad must show what the word means. *Example:* "For the lowest price in town for fossils", visit Rick's Fossil Farm.

Variation: Posters can be made in which the key word is omitted. The children can try and guess what word is being sold.

SORTING WORDS

Places

People

Things

Action Words

Adjectives

Name _____

PRE-READING ACTIVITIES

Card Arrangement I

1. Prior to the lesson, the teacher prepares cards, each containing one event from the reading selection.

2. Using a pocket chart or the chalkrail, have the children discuss in which sequence they believe the events will occur.

3. The class must agree on a final decision.

Note: After reading the selection, the class will want to compare their prediction to the actual sequence of events.

Cut-Ups

The objective of this lesson is to take passages from a story that have been rearranged and put them into a logical order.

1. Before the lesson, the teacher prepares copies of the selection, putting the events in a mixed-up order, similar to Card Arrangement I.

2. Working in groups, the children cut apart the statements and reconstruct them in a meaningful order. The whole group must agree on the order. When a decision has been made, the strips are glued onto a sheet of paper.

3. Compare papers with other groups.

4. After the story has been read, compare the children's sequencing of the story to the actual story that has been read.

Word Substitution

This activity is extremely useful when introducing a theme or topic.

1. The teacher makes up several sentences in which the same key word has been omitted. As each paragraph progresses, each sentence should reveal more about the meaning of the key word.

2. Using an overhead projector the teacher shows the paragraph one sentence at a time. The teacher records several student's responses as they predict what goes in the blanks.

3. As more of the paragraph is revealed, the children may revise, defend or withdraw their guess.

Example: For a unit on friends.

A _____ is a very special thing to have. Everybody needs a _____.

If you have a _____ you can do many things together.

You can go to the park with your _____.

_____ is someone you can play with.

Sometimes your _____ can get you into trouble.

If they are good _____ they don't hurt your feelings.

Your _____ treats you like you are someone special.

A _____ is someone who likes you.

What Do You Know About . . .?

(Use with the reproducible activity sheet found on page 17.)

1. Before starting a theme or story, brainstorm on chart paper or a chalkboard and record answers to the following question "What do you know about..?" Accept and record all the children's answers.

2. Second and third grade children can brainstorm and record their own answers.

Example: If you were reading *Frog and Toad Are Friends*, you would ask the children "What do you know about frogs?

Note: Save the list so when the theme or selection is complete the children can compare pre-knowledge to post-knowledge.

What Does The Title Mean?

(Use with the reproducible activity sheet found on page 18.)

1. Before reading the selection tell the children the title.

2. On large chart paper or on the chalkboard brainstorm what they think the story will be about. Accept all answers. Tell the children they will find out after they read the selection.

3. Second and third grade children can write their own ideas and discuss them orally.

Example: If you were reading *Annie and The Old One*, the children might respond by saying "I think Annie is an old lady and the Old One is an even older lady and they are friends.

What do you know about _____

The title of our new story is: _____

| What do you think the title means? |

_____

_____

_____

_____

_____

_____

_____

_____

Story Detective

The children will look for clues about the story content by examining pictures, chapter titles, and the story title. This can be done in several ways depending on the age of the children and availability of materials.

1. The teacher shows the selection to the children and leads a discussion.

Example:

a) "What do you think a story called _____ would be about?"

b) "You'll be reading a chapter called _____. What do you think will happen in it?"

c) The teacher has several pictures that reveal some of the plot of the story. "What do you think could be happening in this picture?"

Note: All responses can be recorded on chart paper, individually recorded or discussed orally. If individual books are available, the children can be directed to turn to certain pages for activity c.

Read-A-Little-Stop

This activity can be done in two ways.

1. The teacher reads for a short time and then stops at a predetermined place and asks the children how they think the story will end. The children may write down their responses or respond verbally.

2. The children are given the directions to silently read a selection and stop at a predetermined place. Responses can be written or oral.

Guess and Check Illustrations

(Use with the reproducible activity sheet found on page 21.)

1.The teacher gives the children two or three descriptive phrases about a character or the setting from a selection. The children draw a picture that illustrates their interpretation of the phrases.

2. After reading the selection, ask the children to redraw the characters or setting based on their new knowledge. Compare the "guess" with the "check."

Story Title: _____   *Name* _____

Guess ?

Check √

Guess & Check Illustrations

Who Am I?

1. Break the class up into three groups and choose a group leader.

2. Each group leader reads a different prepared statement about the same character in the story. One statement is true and the others are false.

3. After hearing the statements each group prepares an argument to convince the class that their statement is correct. Then the group leader presents the argument to the class and to an impartial person (teacher, aide, parent, principal or student.) The impartial person chooses the group that was the most persuasive. Following this activity the children will read the selection to find out which group had the correct statement.

Sample statements from the story Charlotte's Web

a) My name is Wilbur. I am a farmer who raises corn. My son found a spider who could spin messages in webs.

b) My name is Wilbur. I am a pig who talks. I am very lonely until I meet a spider who becomes my special friend.

c) My name is Wilbur. I am a mouse who lives on the Zuckerman's farm. A spider is teaching me to read by spinning messages in her web.

Note: This activity works best if used with an unfamilar selection.

POST-READING ACTIVITIES

Card Arrangement II

1. The teacher illicits responses from the children in answer to the question, "Tell me one thing that you remember from the story?" All responses are accepted.

2. The teacher writes responses on a large index card or flashcard strip. The teacher returns the card to the student.

3. Repeat until 10 to 12 responses have been given.

4. The children with the cards come up to the front of the classroom.

5. Those children in their seats must decide as a group how they want to arrange the cards in a meaningful way. There must be a consensus among the children. Any arrangement that makes sense and that the group can defend is acceptable.

Postcard

(Use with the reproducible activity sheet found on page 24.)

1. Copy the following activity sheet on heavy construction paper.

2. Have the children write a postcard to
    a) a friend and persuade them to read the story
    b) a movie producer and convince him to make a movie of the story
    c) the author and tell what you liked about the story
    d) to a library and convince them to purchase the book for the
       library shelves.

3. On the other side of the postcard, have the children draw an appropriate illustration.

Dear

Your Friend,

Place
Postage
Stamp
Here

T.S. Denison & Co., Inc.

Postcard Activity

Re-Write The Ending

(Use with the reproducible activity sheet found on page 26.)

1. This activity can be done several ways:

a) Depending on the story, the children can be directed to create a new ending from a certain point in the story and illustrate it.

b) The children take original ending of the story and extend the story beyond the author's ending and illustrate it.

Note: For younger children the teacher can collect ideas for new endings orally.

Star Maps

(Use with the reproducible activity sheet found on page 27.)

1. Have the children list the events, character descriptions or the setting on the Star Map activity sheet.

Example: From the setting of Goldilocks and the Three Bears.

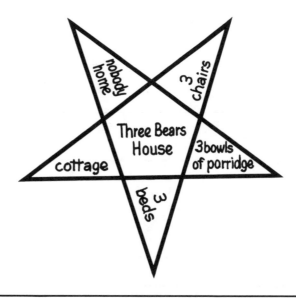

My New Ending of the Story: _____

By: _____

STAR MAPS

Somebody/Wanted/But/So

(Use with the reproducible activity sheet found on page 29.)

1. This is a quick and easy activity used to check the children's understanding of the main idea of the selection.

2. Using the reproducible activity sheet found on page 29, the children should fill in the following categories:

SOMEBODY - indicates the main character in the story.
WANTED and BUT - describes the problem in the story.
SO - is the conclusion or solution.

When finished it should read like a cohesive sentence.

Example from Where The Wild Things Are
Somebody/Wanted/But/So

Max **wanted** to sail away and went to where the wild things are **but** he got tired of being their king and **wanted** to go home **so** he sailed away.

SOMEBODY / WANTED /
BUT / SO The Main Idea of the Selection

Somebody	
Wanted	
But	
So	

Beginning/Middle/End

1. The children fold a large piece of paper into thirds.

2. The sections are labeled beginning, middle and end. The children can:
   a) Draw a picture that shows something that happened at these points in the story, or
   b) Write and draw something that happened at these points in the story.

Story Pyramid

(Use with the reproducible activity sheet found on page 31.)

1. This activity can be done individually, in small groups or as a large group.

2. The pyramid is as follows:
   1) - Name of character
   2) - 2 words describing the setting
   3) - 3 words describing a character
   4) - 4 words in a sentence describing one event
   5) - 5 words in a sentence describing another event

NAME _____

STORY PYRAMID

1 _____

2 _____   _____

3 _____ _____ _____

4 _____ _____ _____ _____

5 _____ _____ _____ _____ _____

DIRECTIONS:

1) 1 word name of a character.

2) 2 words that describe the setting.

3) 3 words that describe a character.

4) 4 words in a sentence that describe one event.

5) 5 words in a sentence that describe another event.

Character Map

(Use with the reproducible activity sheet found on page 33.)

1. Using the reproducible activity sheet, the children write or draw in the square a character from the story.

2. In the rectangles the children list adjectives or qualities that describe the character.

3. In the ovals, the children write examples that support the adjectives.

Example from the story of Cinderella

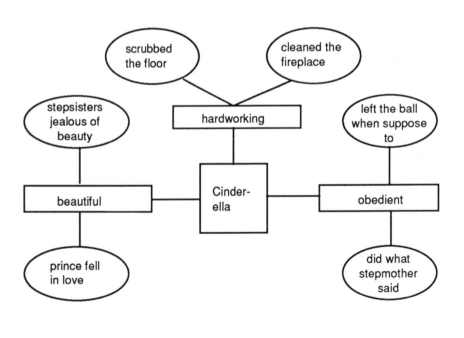

CHARACTER MAP

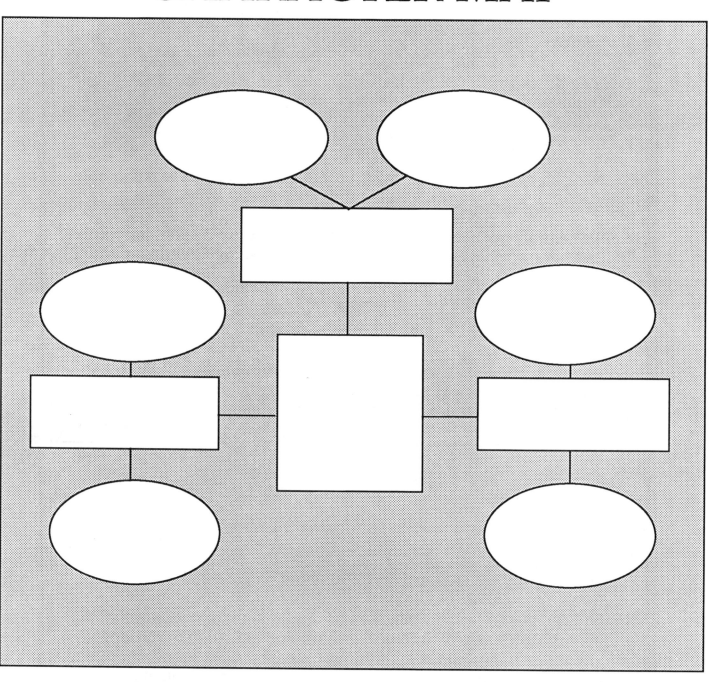

Name of a character.

Qualities that describe the character.

Examples of those qualities.

NAME _____

T.V. Show

1. Using the selection the teacher extracts statements (one statement per child) that advance the plot of the story. Include the title page.

2. The statements are numbered and each child is given one.

3. The children glue their statements on 8.5 x 11 inch paper and illustrate it.

4. All papers are put in order and are taped together to make one long strip. The ends are taped to cardboard tubes as shown in the illustration.

5. Two children turn the tubes in unison so the other children can watch the "T.V. show." A narrator can be used to tell the story. To add to the enjoyment of this activity, the class can make a television from a cardboard box.

Small Talk

(Use with the reproducible activity sheet found on page 35.)

1. The Reproducible activity page can be used in a number of ways:
   a) Two characters from the story can have a conversation by retelling the story.
   b) Two characters from the story are having a conversation about something that could have happened in the story.
   c) The children can pretend that they are conversing with one of the characters from the story.

2. The children fill the dialogue bubbles and illustrate.

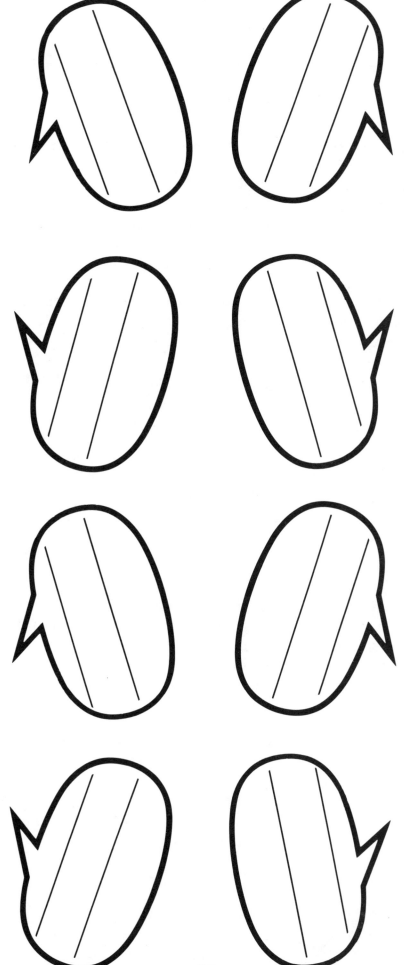

Mural

1. The class needs to be divided into three or more groups.

2. This activity can be done in several ways:

      a) In their groups, the children generate 5 to 10 statements that tell the story. On lined paper they sequence the events and glue them in order onto a large piece of butcher paper above the written statements the children can draw illustrations.

      b) The activity can be accomplished in the same manner with the exception of the teacher helping the children to generate the statements. Each group would order and illustrate the same statements.

3. Younger children can illustrate and tell the teacher what is happening in their picture.

Bookcover

1. On blank paper, the children design a new book cover for the selection that they have been reading or having read to them. It can reflect;
    a) something that has happened in the story,
    b) their favorite part of the story,
    c) their favorite character, or
    d) an appropriate picture for the title of the story.

Take-A-Picture

1. After the selection has been read to the children, ask the children to pretend that they are photographers. They should take a picture of the most important part of the story by drawing it.

2. The children can add a caption to explain what is happening in their photograph.

Map-It-Out

1. Have the children draw a map from;
   a) The "setting" in the story.
   b) The character's neighborhood, city, or room.

Example: Draw a map of the Hundred Acre Wood from *Winnie-The-Pooh*.

Truth or Garbage?

1. The teacher prepares statements about a selection the children have read. Some of the statements are true and some of the statements are false (garbage).

2. The children have a card with the word "truth" written on one side, and the word "garbage" written on the other side. *(Cards can be laminated for durability.)*

3. The children respond to each of the teacher's statements by holding up their card to vote.

Casting Director

1. After the children have read the selection, ask them to list all the characters and discuss their attributes and personality. This can be done individually or as a class.

2. As a casting director, the children will cast the children from their class into the roles of some of the characters from the story. The children should try to cast the children according to similarities they may share with the characters from the story.

3. Those children cast as a character in the story might enjoy trying to dramatize a scene or event from the story.

Venn Diagram

(Use with the reproducible activity sheet found on page 39.)

1. A Venn Diagram is an excellent tool to compare how characters or stories are alike and different. It can be used to compare;
    a) Two characters from the same story.
    b) Two characters that are similar from two different stories.
    c) Plots from two different stories.
    d) Settings from two different stories.

VENN DIAGRAM

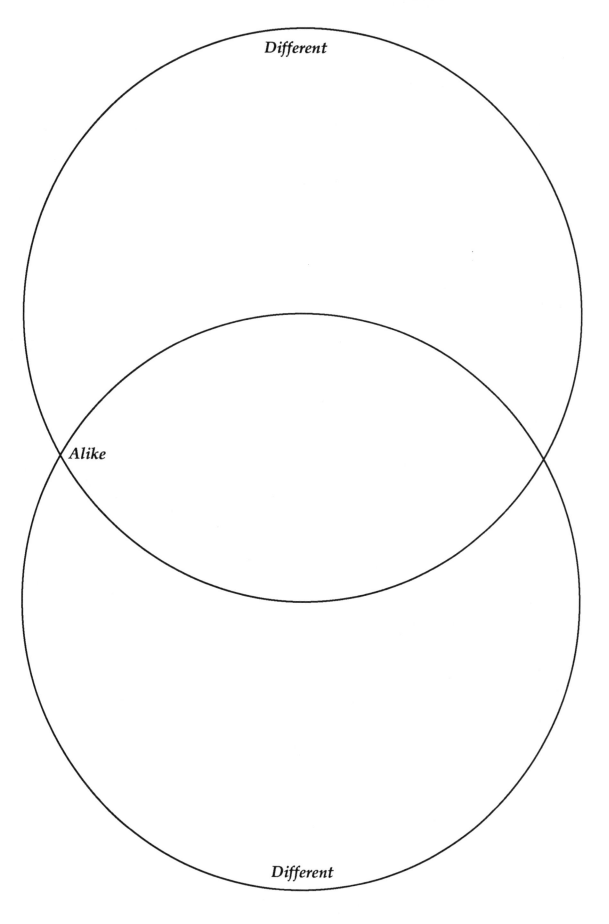

Different

Alike

Different

NAME

Stump The Teacher

1. Before the children read the selection, the teacher tells them that they will be the teacher for today. Their job will be to ask the teacher questions about what has been read.

2. Everytime the class "stumps" the "teacher" they get a point and vise-versa.

Story Squares

(Use with the reproducible activity sheet found on page 41.)

1. This activity can be done as a whole group, small group or individually.

2. Depending on the reading level and ability of the children, the boxes on the activity page can be filled in using words, phrases or sentences to complete the descriptions.

3. The last box can be left up to the discretion of the teacher. Possible ideas for the blank box are;
   a) Wonderful words,
   b) My favorite part,
   c) The scariest part,
   d) The funniest part,
   e) The specific theme or topic your class may be working on.

Story Squares

Setting	Plot

Character 1	Character 2

Character 3	Problem

Solution	

This is my favorite character from the story:

_____

The character's name is _____

_____ is a funny story.
This is a picture of the funniest part of the story.

I thought _____
was a scary story. This is a picture of the
scariest part of the story.

This is a picture of my favorite scene from the story,

_____

Write the most interesting sentence from the story and draw a picture.

Name _____

T.S. Denison & Co., Inc.

Make Your Own Bookmark

Draw a picture that shows something about the story.

Name _____

Draw a picture of the setting and write 2 sentences that describe it.   NAME _____

T.S. Denison & Co., Inc.